The Monkeys Who Tried Kindness

Sally Huss

This book is dedicated to Anaheim, California,
The City of Kindness,
where a culture of kindness was started in 2010.
This has improved the lives of citizens, schools and businesses.
In 2015 Anaheim's elementary school children
completed 1 million acts of kindness, setting an example
for children and adults everywhere.
When kindness rules, every city can become a City of Kindness.

Copyright @2017 Sally Huss
Huss Publishing
All Rights Reserved

ISBN: 10: 1-945742267
ISBN 13: 9781945742262

The Monkeys Who Tried Kindness

A pack of monkeys living in the jungle

Was carrying on in such a jumble!

The Monkeys Who Tried Kindness

They were fighting and biting…

The Monkeys Who Tried Kindness

And swearing and not sharing.

The Monkeys Who Tried Kindness

Oh, oh this was not good.

This was no way to live. It's not like it should.

The Monkeys Who Tried Kindness

Bananas were being taken from some during the darkness of night.

The Monkeys Who Tried Kindness

In the morning once discovered, there'd be a terrible fight.

The Monkeys Who Tried Kindness

A mother had to watch her little one like a hawk

Or it could be snatched away while out for a walk.

Teenagers were up to no good.

They would ransack a nest, breaking everything they could.

The grandparent monkeys seemed to care less

While watching their grandchildren make an awful mess.

Everyone was becoming so selfish and full of fear,

No monkey wanted another monkey near, it was clear.

The Monkeys Who Tried Kindness

On top of that, the monkeys were getting sicker and sicker,

As not one of them wanted to be another's picker.

The Monkeys Who Tried Kindness

You see, monkeys naturally preen and clean each other.

It doesn't matter if it is a stranger, a brother, or a mother.

They pick out the ticks and mites from each other's fur and skin.

In this way no sickness ever settles in.

But in this particular monkey troop,

This lack of hygiene has led them to become a very sickly group.

"What's the trouble? What's gone wrong?

Why can't we get along?"

The Monkeys Who Tried Kindness

This is what each monkey said to himself,

Even as one was stealing something from another's wealth.

The Monkeys Who Tried Kindness

"We've become dreary with worry,

Sick from lack of contact,

A menace to each other and ourselves to boot.

Let's change things," said one monkey, as he dropped some loot.

The Monkeys Who Tried Kindness

Each could see the problem, but could not see the solution.

"Kindness," said a soft, little voice in all of the confusion.

"What? What?" They could not believe their ears.

"What is it that can make us behave and calm our fears?"

"Kindness," repeated the little voice within the din.

"Try kindness," said the youngster again and again.

The Monkeys Who Tried Kindness

"Kindness?" questioned one of the elders.

"It couldn't hurt," said another of the members.

The Monkeys Who Tried Kindness

"Let's try it," one said. "We need a new scheme.

We could always go back to being selfish and mean."

"Agreed! Agreed!" They all agreed to give it a go.

But how would they do it? They were not sure they'd know.

The next day when the sun came out,

They needn't worry, there was little doubt

That this group was on the right path.

Sweet sounds floated through the air, with an occasional laugh.

The Monkeys Who Tried Kindness

Monkeys were sharing the fruit they had found.

The Monkeys Who Tried Kindness

The youngsters were happy together, just monkeying around.

Monkeys scratched each other's backs in the kindest way,
Sending all the mites and ticks, and even loneliness away.

The Monkeys Who Tried Kindness

The grandparents, who had little interest

in their grandchildren before,

Began reading to those youngsters, whom they now so adore.

Kindness works wonders, they all had to agree.

It works in all kinds of situations, they all could now see.

So that's how a troop of silly monkeys found their way back to their natural state.

It was through simple acts of kindness that opened the gate.

The Monkeys Who Tried Kindness

You too may be tempted to do something mean or uncaring.

Try kindness first, you'll feel better for your daring.

The Monkeys Who Tried Kindness

Kindness is not just monkey business, you'll find.

It's everybody's business – to be kind, truly kind.

The end, but not the end of being kind to one another.

Hardly a day goes by in which kindness doesn't make the day better.

At the end of this book you will find a Certificate of Merit that may be issued to any child who has fulfilled the requirements stated in the Certificate. This fine Certificate will easily fit into a 5"x7" frame, and happily suit any girl or boy who receives it!

Sally writes new books all the time. If you would like to be alerted when one of her new books becomes available or when one of her e-books is offered FREE on Amazon, sign up on her website, www.sallyhuss.com.

If you liked *The Monkeys Who Tried Kindness,* please be kind enough to post a short review for it on Amazon. Thank you.

Here are a few Sally Huss books you might enjoy. They may be found on Amazon.

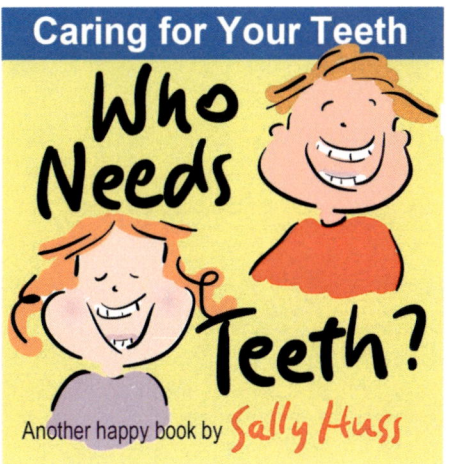

About the Author/Illustrator

"Bright and happy," "light and whimsical" have been the catch phrases attached to the writings and art of Sally Huss for over 30 years. Sweet images dance across all of Sally's creations, whether in the form of children's books, paintings, wallpaper, ceramics, baby bibs, purses, clothing, or her King Features syndicated newspaper panel "Happy Musings."

Sally creates children's books to uplift the lives of children and hopes you will join her in this effort by helping spread her happy messages.

Sally is a graduate of USC with a degree in Fine Art and through the years has had 26 of her own licensed art galleries throughout the world.

Made in the USA
San Bernardino, CA
27 August 2018